May 2012

RECOVERY ACT

Tax Debtors Have Received FHA Mortgage Insurance and First-Time Homebuyer Credits

GAO

Accountability ★ Integrity ★ Reliability

GAO-12-592

May 2012

RECOVERY ACT

Tax Debtors Have Received FHA Mortgage Insurance and First-Time Homebuyer Credits

Why GAO Did This Study

Under a Recovery Act provision that increased mortgage insurance loan limits, FHA insured $20 billion in mortgages for 87,000 homeowners. The Recovery Act also provided for the awarding of an estimated $12 billion of FTHBCs to 1.7 million individuals. GAO was asked to determine the (1) extent to which tax debtors benefited from the Recovery Act's provisions for increased FHA loan limits and the FTHBC, and (2) challenges, if any, FHA faces in preventing ineligible tax debtors from receiving mortgage insurance. Using IRS and FHA data, GAO identified Recovery Act recipients and compared them to federal tax debtors as of June 30, 2010. GAO reviewed relevant policies and interviewed agency officials and lenders. GAO also reviewed detailed IRS and FHA documents for a nonrepresentative selection of 18 individuals who received FHA mortgage insurance. These were selected based on a combination of factors, such as amount of taxes owed and number of delinquent tax periods. Due to data availability and other factors, GAO was able to completely evaluate only 8 of 18 individuals on their eligibility for FHA mortgage insurance. These cases cannot be generalized beyond those presented.

What GAO Recommends

HUD should (1) consult with IRS to require lenders to collect more reliable tax debt information from applicants and (2) provide lenders with revised policies or guidance, including the consideration of tax liens, for approving FHA mortgage insurance. HUD agreed with the recommendations.

View GAO-12-592. For more information, contact Greg Kutz at (202) 512-6722 or kutzg@gao.gov.

What GAO Found

The Federal Housing Administration (FHA) insured over $1.44 billion in mortgages for 6,327 borrowers with $77.6 million in federal tax debt who benefited from the 2009 American Recovery and Reinvestment Act. Of these borrowers, 3,815 individuals claimed and received $27.4 million in Recovery Act First-Time Homebuyer Credits (FTHBC). This analysis includes tax debtors who (1) benefited from FHA's increased loan limits, or (2) claimed the FTHBCs and received FHA mortgage insurance of any value. Federal policy makes delinquent tax debtors ineligible for FHA mortgage insurance unless they repay their debt or are in a valid repayment agreement with the Internal Revenue Service (IRS), but the FTHBC, like all tax credits, was available to those who qualified, regardless of their tax debt. GAO could not determine the proportion of borrowers who were ineligible for FHA insurance because GAO could not systematically identify which of the 6,327 borrowers were in valid repayment agreements using the data GAO received from IRS. However, GAO did find that 5 of the 8 borrowers completely evaluated were ineligible because they were not in valid repayment agreements at the time they obtained FHA mortgage insurance. In addition, GAO found that Recovery Act borrowers with unpaid taxes had foreclosure rates two to three times greater than borrowers without unpaid taxes, which potentially represents an increased risk to FHA.

Some ineligible tax debtors received FHA mortgage insurance, in part, due to shortcomings in the capacity of FHA-required documentation to identify tax debts, and shortcomings in other policies that lenders may misinterpret. Lenders must perform steps to identify an applicant's federal debt status, but sources commonly used, such as the loan application and credit report, do not reliably indicate an applicant's tax debt. Statutory restrictions generally prohibit the disclosure of taxpayer information, such as tax debt, without the taxpayer's consent. Lenders are already required to obtain such consent through an IRS form they use to validate the income of some applicants. This same form could also be used to obtain permission from applicants to obtain reliable tax-debt information directly from IRS, but doing so is not addressed in FHA policies. Requiring lenders to collect more reliable information on tax debts could better prevent ineligible tax debtors from obtaining FHA mortgage insurance. Further, FHA's policies requiring lenders to investigate whether tax liens indicate unresolved tax debt are unclear and may be misinterpreted. The lenders GAO spoke with believed they were in compliance with FHA's policies when they provided FHA-insured loans to applicants with tax liens and no repayment agreements, but FHA officials indicated otherwise. As a result of these shortcomings, lenders may approve federally insured mortgages for ineligible applicants with delinquent tax debt in violation of federal policies.

_____ United States Government Accountability Office

Contents

Abbreviations

CAIVRS	Credit Alert Interactive Voice Response System
CBO	Congressional Budget Office
ESA	Economic Stimulus Act
FHA	Federal Housing Administration
FTHBC	First-Time Homebuyer Credit
HAIA	Homebuyer Assistance and Improvement Act
HERA	Housing and Economic Recovery Act
HUD	Department of Housing and Urban Development
IRS	Internal Revenue Service
IVES	Income Verification Express Service
LI	Lender Insurance
MMIF	Mutual Mortgage Insurance Fund
OMB	Office of Management and Budget
SFDW	Single Family Data Warehouse
SSN	Social Security number
TIN	Taxpayer Identification Number
TOTAL	Technology Open to Approved Lenders
URLA	Uniform Residential Loan Application

This is a work of the U.S. government and is not subject to copyright protection in the United States. The published product may be reproduced and distributed in its entirety without further permission from GAO. However, because this work may contain copyrighted images or other material, permission from the copyright holder may be necessary if you wish to reproduce this material separately.

United States Government Accountability Office
Washington, DC 20548

May 29, 2012

Congressional Requesters

As of September 30, 2011, individuals, businesses, and other entities owed the U.S. government over $350 billion in known unpaid taxes, including interest and penalties, according to the Internal Revenue Service (IRS).[1] Beyond this amount of known tax debt, the amount of unknown tax debts is substantial. This is because the inventory of tax debts excludes underreported amounts filed by taxpayers and taxes owed by taxpayers who do not file tax returns.[2] Given the many challenges that IRS faces, the enforcement of the tax laws continues to be on our list of high-risk areas.[3] We have previously reported that many individuals with tax debt take advantage of government programs, such as federal loan insurance, thereby reaping benefits from these programs while failing to pay their own taxes.[4]

The American Recovery and Reinvestment Act of 2009 included numerous provisions aimed at spurring economic activity and shoring up the declining housing market. Under a provision that increased the maximum loan limits for mortgage insurance in 2009, the Federal Housing Administration (FHA), part of the Department of Housing and Urban Development (HUD), insured more than $20 billion in mortgages

---

[1]This figure includes (1) taxes receivable of $147 billion, (2) compliance assessments—amounts that have not been agreed to by either the taxpayer or a court—of $103 billion, and (3) write-offs of $106 billion.

[2]In addition to known unpaid taxes, the net tax gap, estimated to be about $385 billion for tax year 2006 (the most recent estimate made), represents the net amount of noncompliance with the tax laws (after enforcement and late payments). According to IRS, underreporting of tax liability accounts for 84 percent of the gross gap, and nonfiling and underpayment of taxes comprised the rest of the gross tax gap. Tax gap estimates do not include all areas of the economy, such as illegal activity.

[3]GAO, 2011 High-Risk Series: An Update, GAO-11-278 (Washington, D.C.: February 2011).

[4]GAO, Debt Collection: Barring Delinquent Taxpayers From Receiving Federal Contracts and Loan Assistance, GAO/T-GGD/AIMD-00-167 (Washington D.C.: May 9, 2000); and Management Report: Improvements Are Needed to Enhance the Internal Revenue Service's Internal Controls and Operating Effectiveness, GAO-11-494R (Washington, D.C.: June 21, 2011).

for 87,000 borrowers.[5] In addition, as of July 3, 2010, over 1.7 million individuals were awarded over $12 billion in First-Time Homebuyer Credits (FTHBC) under the Recovery Act for homes purchased in 2009, according to IRS.[6,7] In this report, we refer to individuals who received either increased limits on their FHA mortgage insurance or the FTHBC in 2009 as Recovery Act beneficiaries.

Federal policy makes delinquent tax debtors ineligible for FHA mortgage insurance at the time of application, unless they repaid the debt or were in a valid repayment agreement with IRS, while the FTHBC, like all tax credits, was available to those who qualified regardless of their tax debt. The Recovery Act made no exceptions to these federal policies. You asked us to review several issues concerning individuals with unpaid federal taxes who benefited from the Recovery Act. This is the second in a series of reports that respond to your request. In the first report, we identified thousands of Recovery Act contract and grant recipients that owed hundreds of millions of dollars in federal taxes.[8] In this report, we determined the (1) extent to which tax debtors benefited from the Recovery Act's provisions for increased FHA loan limits and the FTHBC, and (2) challenges, if any, FHA faces in preventing ineligible tax debtors from receiving mortgage insurance.

To determine the extent to which Recovery Act beneficiaries with unpaid tax debt benefitted from the increased loan limits for FHA mortgage insurance or were awarded the FTHBC, we obtained and analyzed FHA mortgage insurance data as of September 2011, IRS data on FTHBC transactions as of July 2010,[9] and IRS data on unpaid federal tax debts

---

[5]We refer to individuals who received FHA mortgage insurance as borrowers.

[6]The Recovery Act FTHBC only covered home purchases from January 1 through November 30, 2009.

[7]GAO, *Tax Administration: Usage and Selected Analyses of the First-Time Homebuyer Credit*, GAO-10-1025R (Washington, D.C.: Sept. 2, 2010).

[8]GAO, *Recovery Act: Thousands of Recovery Act Contract and Grant Recipients Owe Hundreds of Millions in Federal Taxes*, GAO-11-485 (Washington, D.C.: Apr. 28, 2011).

[9]The FTHBC under the Recovery Act had to be claimed on either a 2008 or 2009 tax return. Because returns for the 2009 tax year were due by April 15, 2010, all claims filed on time without an extension would be accounted for in the July 2010 data.

as of June 2010.[10] The FHA data allowed us to identify all those who received FHA insurance under the Recovery Act's increased loan limits. However, limitations in the FTHBC data we received from IRS did not allow us to isolate all individuals who benefited from the FTHBC under the Recovery Act.[11] To address this limitation, we used the FHA data to assist us in isolating FTHBCs awarded under the Recovery Act. As a result, we were unable to analyze any credits for individuals who did not use FHA mortgage insurance in the financing of their home, and therefore we estimate that our analysis included 43 percent of all FTHBCs awarded under the Recovery Act. Our analysis includes two groups:

1. individuals who received FHA mortgage insurance under the higher limits authorized under the Recovery Act, and
2. individuals who received the FTHBC under the Recovery Act and obtained FHA mortgage insurance of any value.

We electronically matched IRS tax debt data to these groups using Social Security numbers (SSN) as unique identifiers. We included only those individuals with tax debts of $100 or more from tax years 2008 and earlier to eliminate small tax debts and debts that may involve matters that are routinely resolved between the taxpayers and IRS, with the taxes paid or abated within a short time. We excluded any debts that were assessed by IRS after the mortgage insurance was received because those debts would not have been included in IRS records at the time the mortgage insurance was issued. We determined that the data were sufficiently reliable to address the report's objectives by performing electronic testing

---

[10]For this analysis we used known federal tax debts. Under federal accounting standards, unpaid tax assessments require agreement from either the taxpayer or the court to be considered federal taxes receivable. Compliance assessments and memo accounts are not considered federal taxes receivable because they are not agreed to by taxpayers or the courts.

[11]IRS's FTHBC data do not contain home purchase dates, which were needed to associate the credit with its enacting legislation. The Recovery Act applied to only 1 of the 3 years for which the FTHBC was available. To obtain the needed dates, we used the Social Security number from the IRS FTHBC data as a unique identifier, and we electronically matched them to Social Security numbers found in the FHA data, which contained home purchase dates. Using this method, we estimate that our analysis included 43 percent of all FTHBCs awarded under the Recovery Act because we were unable to analyze any credits for individuals who did not use FHA mortgage insurance in the financing of their home. Such individuals may have financed their home purchases through conventional loans or other government loan programs, such as those available through the Department of Veterans Affairs.

on the data, speaking with agency officials, and reconciling data to published figures and source documents.

To determine if FHA mortgage insurance was provided to ineligible individuals with unpaid federal tax debt, we identified a nonrepresentative selection of 18 individuals from the above analyses, who had federal tax debt and benefitted from the Recovery Act, for detailed reviews. We selected these individuals based on a combination of (1) high amounts of unpaid federal taxes, (2) at least three delinquent tax periods,[12] (3) an insured mortgage of at least $200,000, and (4) indications of IRS penalties or home foreclosures.[13] We requested IRS notes, detailed account transcripts, and other records from IRS as well as mortgage files from FHA for these 18 individuals. Of these requested cases, FHA provided us information that allowed us to fully analyze 8.[14,15] Although we did not receive complete information necessary to fully analyze the remaining cases, we were able to assess all 18 for limited purposes (e.g., nonfiling of tax returns). We also selected 9 additional cases of FTHBC recipients who received tax refunds to determine how they were able to receive federal tax refunds while having unpaid federal taxes.[16,17] These

---

[12]The length of a delinquent tax period is dependent on the type of tax owed. For instance, income taxes are assessed annually; payroll taxes are assessed quarterly.

[13]The value of mortgage insurance was not a criterion in selecting cases for borrowers who obtained FHA mortgage insurance under the Recovery Act because all of these mortgages resulted from increased FHA loan limits in high-cost areas. For each of the two groups included in our analysis, we selected two cases with IRS civil penalties for noncompliance and two cases in which the home had been foreclosed.

[14]To mask the identities of the tax debtors included in our case studies, we requested additional files from FHA that were not tax debtors.

[15]FHA and IRS provided us some information on an additional three cases; however, we found that two of these cases did not have outstanding debt at the time they obtained FHA mortgage insurance, because they were either deemed an innocent spouse (granted relief from a joint tax liability) or had satisfied the repayment portion on an offer in compromise (an agreement to settle the debt for less than the amount owed). The third case's debt had been removed from IRS because it was beyond the 10-year statutory collection period at the time we received the IRS records, therefore we did not include them in our analysis. We did not receive FHA mortgage files from FHA for the remaining seven case because the lenders for these files had either gone out of business or were not otherwise required to provide the mortgage file, according to FHA officials.

[16]We did not request FHA mortgage files for these nine cases.

[17]Federal law typically requires that any federal tax refund be offset to pay down an individual's unpaid taxes.

cases were selected to illustrate the sizeable amounts of taxes owed by some individuals who benefitted from the Recovery Act but cannot be generalized beyond the cases presented.

To understand how private lenders interpret and implement FHA's guidelines for preventing individuals with delinquent federal tax debt from receiving mortgage insurance, we interviewed FHA officials and reviewed relevant federal laws and policies, FHA regulations, policy manuals, and other FHA documents related to mortgage insurance. We also interviewed officials from three large, private, FHA-approved lenders, which together endorsed 15 percent of all FHA mortgages for homes purchased in 2009, and reviewed and discussed their policies for determining FHA mortgage insurance applicants' tax debt status and preventing ineligible tax debtors from obtaining FHA mortgage insurance. A more detailed description of the scope and methodology can be found in appendix I.

We conducted this performance audit from April 2011 through May 2012 in accordance with generally accepted government auditing standards. Those standards require that we plan and perform the audit to obtain sufficient, appropriate evidence to provide a reasonable basis for our audit findings and conclusions based on our audit objectives. We believe that the evidence obtained provides a reasonable basis for our findings and conclusions based on our audit objectives.

Background

The Recovery Act of 2009 was enacted in response to significant weakness in the economy to, among other things, help promote economic recovery and assist those most affected by the recession.[18] The Congressional Budget Office (CBO) estimated the Recovery Act's cost at $825 billion as of August 2011. The Recovery Act included provisions to help stimulate the housing market, including increasing loan limits for FHA-insured mortgages in 669 high-cost counties in calendar year 2009.[19] The provision allowed FHA to insure mortgages at a higher amount than would have been authorized without the Recovery Act. Under this provision, FHA insured over $20 billion in mortgages for 87,000 homeowners who were approved for FHA mortgage insurance in 2009. The Recovery Act also adapted and extended the FTHBC through

---

[18]Pub. L. No. 111-5 (Feb. 17, 2009).

[19]Section 1202 of Pub. L. No. 111-5.

November 2009.[20] Through July 3, 2010, IRS reported that about 1.7 million individuals claimed more than $12 billion in FTHBCs under the Recovery Act for homes purchased in 2009.[21] Office of Management and Budget (OMB) Circular A-129 states that delinquent tax debtors are ineligible for federal loan insurance, such as FHA mortgage insurance, unless they repaid the debt or were in a valid repayment agreement with IRS, but the FTHBC was available to those who qualified regardless of their tax debt.

FHA Mortgage Insurance

FHA's single-family programs insure private lenders against 100 percent of the value of the loan for foreclosures on mortgages that meet FHA criteria, including mortgages for initial home purchases, construction rehabilitation, and refinancing. As of September 2011, almost 3,700 lenders were approved to participate in these programs.[22] The insurance covers the principal, interest, and associated foreclosure costs, among other things.[23] Lenders usually require mortgage insurance when a home buyer makes a down payment of less than 20 percent of the value of the home. FHA mortgage insurance allows a home buyer to make a modest down payment—as low as 3.5 percent—and obtain a mortgage for the balance of the purchase price. As the recent housing and economic recession set in, FHA's share of the market for home purchase mortgages grew sharply due to the contraction of other mortgage market segments—rising from about 5 percent in 2006 to nearly 30 percent in

---

[20]The FTHBC was originally enacted by the Housing and Economic Recovery Act of 2008 (HERA) as an interest free loan of up to $7,500 and was to expire on July 1, 2009. Pub. L. No. 110-289, § 3011 (July 30, 2008). The Recovery Act modified and extended the FTHBC by increasing the maximum refundable credit to $8,000 for homes purchases from January 1, 2009, through November 30, 2009, with no payback required unless the home ceases to be the taxpayer's principal residence within 3 years of the purchase. Pub. L. No. 111-5, § 1006 (Feb. 17, 2009).

[21]Homes purchased in 2009 would have been claimed on tax returns filed in 2009 or 2010.

[22]Prior to January 1, 2011, about 13,000 lending institutions were approved to participate in FHA's single-family mortgage insurance programs. At that time, FHA stopped allowing loan correspondents to participate in FHA programs. Loan correspondents were lenders that originated FHA-insured loans—meaning that they could accept mortgage applications, obtain employment verifications and credit histories on applicants, order appraisals, and perform other tasks that precede the loan underwriting process—but did not have direct endorsement authority.

[23]24 C.F.R. § 203.402.

2009.[24,25] FHA insured almost 2 million single-family mortgages valued at more than $300 billion in mortgage insurance in 2009.[26] FHA generally is thought to promote stability in the market by ensuring the availability of mortgage credit in areas that may be underserved by the private sector or that are experiencing economic downturns. It has played a particularly large role among minority, lower-income, and first-time home buyers; almost 80 percent of FHA-insured home purchase loans in 2010 went to first-time home buyers.[27,28]

The FHA home mortgage insurance programs are funded by the FHA Mutual Mortgage Insurance Fund (MMIF), which is supported by insurance premiums charged to borrowers. The MMIF is used to cover claims on foreclosed mortgages, among other things. The Omnibus Budget Reconciliation Act of 1990 required the Secretary of HUD to take steps to ensure that the MMIF attained a capital ratio (i.e., economic value divided by the unamortized insurance-in-force) of at least 2 percent by November 2000 and maintain a 2 percent ratio at all times thereafter.[29] The act also required an annual independent actuarial review of the economic net worth and soundness of the MMIF. The actuarial review estimates the economic value of the MMIF as well as the capital ratio to determine whether the MMIF has met the capital standards in the act. The capital ratio has dropped sharply in recent years due to declines in home prices and increases in seriously delinquent loans and foreclosures. The most recent actuarial study shows that the capital ratio is currently below the statutorily mandated level, at 0.24 percent, representing $2.6 billion in estimated capital resources against an active

---

[24]In fiscal year 2011, FHA's share of the market for home purchases was about 24 percent.

[25]GAO, *Mortgage Financing: Opportunities to Enhance Management and Oversight of FHA's Financial Condition,* GAO-10-827R (Washington D.C.: Sept. 14, 2010).

[26]FHA, *Annual Management Report Fiscal Year 2009* (Washington D.C.: 2009).

[27]HUD generally defines a first-time homebuyer as an individual who has had no ownership in a principal residence during the 3-year period ending on the date of purchase of the property.

[28]See GAO-10-827R.

[29]12 U.S.C. § 1711.

portfolio of $1.08 trillion.[30] The MMIF has historically been sufficient to fund the FHA home mortgage insurance programs without additional funding from the federal government, but if the reserve were to be depleted, FHA would need to draw on permanent and indefinite budget authority to cover additional increases in estimated losses. A weakening in the performance of FHA-insured loans could increase the possibility that FHA will require additional federal funds. Our work has previously shown that the increased reliance on FHA mortgage insurance highlights the need for FHA to ensure that it has the proper controls in place to minimize financial risks to the federal government while meeting the housing needs of borrowers.[31]

Lenders are responsible for underwriting the loans to determine an applicant's eligibility for FHA mortgage insurance in accordance with FHA policies. Underwriting is a risk analysis that uses information collected during the loan origination process to decide whether to approve a loan for FHA insurance. Lenders employ automated underwriting— the process by which lenders enter information on potential borrowers into electronic systems that contain an evaluative formula, or algorithm, known as a scorecard. The scorecard attempts to quickly and objectively measure the borrower's risk of default by examining data such as application information and credit score.[32] Since 2004, FHA has used its own scorecard called Technology Open to Approved Lenders (TOTAL). FHA lenders now use TOTAL in conjunction with automated underwriting systems to determine the likelihood of default. Although TOTAL can assess the credit risk of a borrower, it does not reject a loan outright. Rather, TOTAL will assign a risk assessment of either "accept" or "refer" for each borrower. FHA requires lenders to manually underwrite loans that are assessed as "refer" by TOTAL to give a final determination if the loan should be accepted or rejected. According to FHA policy, a lender

---

[30]HUD, *Annual Report to Congress, Fiscal Year 2011 Financial Status, FHA Mutual Mortgage Insurance Fund* (Nov. 15, 2011), p. 33, http://portal.hud.gov/hudportal/documents/huddoc?id=FHAMMIFundAnnRptFY2011.pdf.

[31]GAO, *Federal Housing Administration: Improvements Needed in Risk Assessment and Human Capital Management*, GAO-12-15 (Washington, D.C.: Nov. 7, 2011).

[32]Credit scores assign a numeric value generally ranging from 300-850 to a borrower's credit history, with higher values signifying better credit. Per FHA policy, applicants with credit scores below 500 are not qualified for FHA mortgage insurance.

remains accountable for compliance with FHA eligibility requirements, regardless of the risk assessment provided by TOTAL.

Virtually all of the lenders that participate in FHA's mortgage insurance programs for single-family homes have direct endorsement authority. These lenders can underwrite and close mortgage loans without FHA's prior review or approval.[33] FHA insures lenders against nearly all losses resulting from foreclosed loans and covers 100 percent of the value of the loan. In general, foreclosure may be initiated when three monthly installments are due and unpaid, and it must be initiated when six monthly installments are due and unpaid, except when prohibited by law.[34] To minimize the number of FHA loans entering foreclosure, servicers are responsible for pursuing various loss mitigation strategies, including suspended payments, loan modification, reduced mortgage payments, and sale of the property by the borrower. If, despite these loss mitigation strategies, the lender forecloses on the loan, the lender can file an insurance claim with FHA for the unpaid balance of the loan and other costs.[35] However, FHA reviews a selection of insured loans, including early payment defaults (loans at least 60 days delinquent in the first six payments), in part to minimize potential FHA losses and ensure the underwriting for these mortgages met FHA guidelines. Reviews revealing serious deficiencies may result in FHA requiring the lenders to compensate the department for financial losses, known as indemnification, which requires the lender to repay FHA for any losses that it incurs after a loan has gone into default and the property has been sold.

Congress, through legislation, sets limits on the size of loans that may be insured by FHA. These loan limits vary by county and can change from year to year. To mitigate the effects from the economic downturn and the sharp reduction of mortgage credit availability from private sources,

---

[33]According to FHA officials, direct endorsement lenders who participate in FHA's lender insurance (LI) program can underwrite, close, and insure loans while those lenders without LI can underwrite and close loans, but FHA is still responsible for insuring the loans.

[34]24 C.F.R. § 203.606. State law may prohibit the start of foreclosure proceedings within the time frame specified by HUD. Also, military service of the borrower may delay foreclosure proceedings (24 C.F.R. § 203.346).

[35]24 C.F.R. § 203.401.

Congress increased FHA loan limits. The Economic Stimulus Act (ESA) enacted in February 2008 stipulated that FHA loan limits be set temporarily at 125 percent of the median house price in each area,[36] with a maximum loan limit of $729,750 for a one-unit home.[37] Immediately prior to ESA's enactment, the limits had been set at 95 percent of area median house prices.[38] In July 2008, 5 months after passing ESA, Congress passed the Housing and Economic Recovery Act (HERA), which established new statutory limits of 115 percent of area median home prices.[39,40] Then, in February 2009, Congress passed the Recovery Act, which stipulated that FHA loan limits for 2009 be set in each county at the higher dollar amount when comparing loan limits established under 2008 ESA requirements and limits for 2009 under HERA.

First-Time Homebuyer Credit

Congress passed the FTHBC to assist the struggling real estate market and encourage individuals to purchase their first home.[41] The credit was initially enacted by HERA and later revised by the Recovery Act. The 2008 HERA FTHBC provided taxpayers a credit of up to $7,500 to be paid back over 15 years, essentially serving as an interest-free loan. In 2009, the Recovery Act was enacted and increased the maximum credit for the 2009 FTHBC to $8,000, with no payback required unless the home is sold or ceases to be the taxpayer's principal residence within 3 years of

---

[36]Pub. L. No. 110-185, § 202 (Feb. 13, 2008).

[37]Loan limits for one- through four-unit homes under ESA were $729,750, $934,200, $1,129,250, and $1,403,400, respectively.

[38]In 2007, the loan limits were 95 percent of the local median home price, with a maximum loan limit of $362,790 for one-unit homes. Limits for one- through four-unit homes were $362,790, $464,449, $561,441, and $697,696, respectively.

[39]Pub. L. No. 110-289, § 2111 (July 30, 2008). Loan limits for one- through four-unit homes under HERA were $625,500, $800,775, $967,950, and $1,202,925, respectively.

[40]Although loan limits under HERA were to be effective in 2009, they were not fully implemented due to a series of temporary measures passed by Congress, including the Recovery Act, to ensure the higher limits were allowed to continue.

[41]Under 26 U.S.C. § 36, a first-time home buyer has not had an ownership interest in any principal residence during the 3-year period prior to the date of the purchase of the home eligible for the credit. No credit is allowed for property (1) located outside the United States, (2) inherited, (3) purchased from a close relative, or (4) purchased by a nonresident alien.

the purchase.[42,43] The credit of up to $8,000 was a refundable tax credit paid out to the claimant if there was no tax liability or the credit exceeded the amount of any federal tax due. In July 2010, the Homebuyer Assistance and Improvement Act (HAIA) of 2010 extended the date to close on a home purchase to September 30, 2010.[44]

Federal Policies on Tax Debtors Receiving Federal Loan Insurance

To protect federal government assets and minimize unintended costs to the government, OMB Circular A-129 states that individuals with delinquent federal debts are ineligible for loan insurance and prohibits federal agencies from issuing loans to such applicants; however, OMB's policy allows individuals with delinquent federal taxes or other federal debt to attain eligibility by repaying their debt in full or entering into a valid repayment plan with the agency they owe.[45] The policy states that agencies should determine if the applicant is eligible by including a question on loan applications asking applicants if they have such delinquencies. The policy also (1) requires agencies and lenders to use credit bureaus as screening tools, because tax liens resulting from delinquent tax debt typically appear on credit reports, and (2) encourages agencies to use HUD's Credit Alert Interactive Voice Response System (CAIVRS), a database of delinquent federal debtors. CAIVRS contains delinquent debt information for six federal agencies; however, it does not contain any tax debts from IRS.[46] According to OMB policy, if delinquent federal debts are discovered, processing of applications must be suspended until the applicant attains eligibility.

---

[42]The 2008 FTHBC applies to purchases made from April 9, 2008, through December 31, 2008. The 2008 FTHBC was amended by the 2009 credit, and applies to purchases made from January 1, 2009, through November 30, 2009.

[43]The recapture provision is limited to the amount of gain on the sale, meaning a taxpayer could sell within 3 years and still not be required to make any repayments if the house was not sold for a gain. 26 U.S.C. § 36(f)(3).

[44]Pub. L. No. 111-198 (July 2, 2010). The FTHBC has now expired.

[45]OMB Circular A-129, *Policies for Federal Credit Programs and Non-Tax Receivables,* Appendix A § III (A)(1)(b).

[46]The six agencies that submit delinquent debt information to CAIVRS are: (1) Department of Agriculture, (2) Department of Education, (3) Department of Justice, (4) Department of Housing and Urban Development, (5) Department of Veterans Affairs, and (6) Small Business Administration.

FHA's policies for lenders dictate that an FHA mortgage insurance applicant must be rejected if he or she is delinquent on any federal debt, including tax debt, or has a lien placed against his or her property for a debt owed to the federal government.[47] Like OMB's policy, FHA policy states that an applicant with federal debt may become eligible for mortgage insurance by repaying the debt in full or by entering into a valid repayment agreement with the federal agency owed, which must be verified in writing. Such repayment plans include IRS-accepted installment agreements and offers in compromise.[48] To identify individuals with tax debt, FHA requires mortgage insurance applicants to declare whether they are delinquent or in default on any federal debt on their insurance application, the Uniform Residential Loan Application (URLA). As printed on the application, knowingly making any false statement on the URLA is a federal crime punishable by fine or imprisonment.[49] FHA also requires that lenders review credit reports for all applicants to identify tax liens and other potential derogatory credit information.

FHA Insured over $1.44 Billion in Mortgages for Thousands of Recovery Act Beneficiaries with Federal Tax Debt

In 2009, FHA insured over $1.44 billion in mortgages for 6,327 borrowers who at the same time had delinquent tax debt and benefited from the Recovery Act. According to IRS records, these borrowers had an estimated $77.6 million in unpaid federal taxes as of June 30, 2010. As figure 1 illustrates, our analysis included tax debtors who either benefited from FHA's increased loan limits or who claimed the FTHBC and received FHA mortgage insurance of any value.[50] Although federal policies did not prohibit tax debtors from claiming the FTHBC, they were ineligible for FHA mortgage insurance unless their delinquent federal taxes and other federal debt had been fully repaid or otherwise addressed through a repayment agreement. We could not determine the proportion of

---

[47]HUD Handbook 4155.1, *Mortgage Credit Analysis for Mortgage Insurance* (March 2011).

[48]An offer in compromise is an agreement between a tax debtor and IRS that resolves the tax debtor's tax debt by accepting less than full payment.

[49]18 U.S.C. § 1001.

[50]Limitations with the FTHBC data we obtained from IRS required that we analyze FTHBCs for home buyers who also obtained FHA mortgage insurance—or approximately 43 percent of all Recovery Act FTHBCs. Therefore, we were unable to identify FTHBCs for those who purchased their homes using cash, conventional mortgages, or other means. See appendix I for additional details on this limitation.

borrowers who were ineligible because we could not systematically identify which of the 6,327 borrowers had valid repayment agreements at the time of the mortgage approval using IRS's data; however, we found that five of our eight selected borrowers were not in valid repayment agreements at the time they obtained FHA mortgage insurance. In addition, FHA records indicate that borrowers with tax debt had serious delinquency (in default for 90 days or more) and foreclosure rates two to three times greater than borrowers without tax debt, which potentially represents an increased risk to FHA.[51]

---

[51]A mortgage is considered delinquent any time a payment is due and not paid. Once the borrower is 30 days late in making a payment, FHA considers the mortgage to be in default. Once the mortgage has been in default for 90 days or more it is considered to be seriously delinquent.

GAO-12-592 Recovery Act

Figure 1: Tax Debtors who Benefitted from the Recovery Act Obtained $1.44 Billion in FHA Mortgage Insurance and $27.4 Million in FTHBCs

Benefit tax debtor received	Number of tax debtors	Amount of known unpaid tax debt	Federal benefits to individuals with known federal tax debt	
			FHA mortgage insurance	FTHBC
FHA Mortgage Insurance under the Recovery Act	2,646[a]	$35.5 million	$759.3 million	N/A
FTHBCs from the IRS under the Recovery Act and FHA Mortgage Insurance	3,815[b]	$43.5 million	$717.2 million	$27.4 million[c]
Overlap (Both FTHBC and FHA Mortgage Insurance under the Recovery Act)	(134)	($1.4 million)	($36.5 million)	(N/A)
Total	**6,327**	**$77.6 million**	**$1.44 billion**	**$27.4 million**

Source: GAO analysis of FHA mortgage data as of September 2011, IRS FTHBC data as of July 10, 2010, and IRS known tax debt data as of June 30, 2010.

[a] 3.7% of all Recovery Act mortgages.

[b] 0.5% of all FHA insured mortgages for borrowers who also claimed the FTHBC.

[c] The FTHBC, like all tax credits, was available to those who qualified, regardless of their tax debt.

Note: We cannot determine the proportion of borrowers who were ineligible for mortgage insurance because we could not systematically identify which of the 6,327 borrowers had valid repayment agreements using the data we received from IRS.

FHA Insured $759.3 Million in Mortgages for Tax Debtors Benefitting from the Recovery Act's Increased Loan Limits

In 2009, FHA insured $759.3 million in mortgages for 2,646 individuals who owed $35.5 million in unpaid federal taxes as of June 30, 2010, under the Recovery Act's provision for increased loan limits.[52] These borrowers and coborrowers obtained 1,913 insured mortgages with a median value of $352,309 and had a median tax debt of $6,290 per person.[53] Their mortgages accounted for 3.7 percent of the 52,006 mortgages FHA insured under Recovery Act provisions for increased limits in 2009, which in turn represented 2.5 percent of all mortgages insured by FHA in 2009. Our analysis likely understates the amount of unpaid federal taxes because IRS data do not cover individuals who fail to file tax returns or who understate their income. Of the 18 selected individuals who benefitted from increased loan limits for FHA mortgage insurance or received the FTHBC under the Recovery Act, we found that 11 had not filed all of their federal tax returns.

Using IRS data, we cannot systematically determine which of these individuals was in a valid repayment agreement at the time of the mortgage, and therefore cannot determine whether insuring each of these 1,913 mortgages was improper, but it is possible that borrowers with tax debt represent a greater financial risk to the federal government.[54] As illustrated in figure 2, serious delinquency and foreclosure rates among Recovery Act borrowers with unpaid federal taxes were at least twice as

---

[52]Our analysis of Recovery Act mortgage insurance borrowers with tax debt as of June 30, 2010, excluded (1) tax debts that have not been agreed to by the tax debtor or affirmed by the court (i.e., tax debts that IRS classified as compliance assessments or memo accounts for financial reporting), (2) tax debts from calendar year 2009 and 2010 tax periods, (3) tax debts that were assessed by IRS after the mortgage insurance was issued, and (4) tax debts of less than $100. Additionally, there is generally a 10-year statutory collection period beyond which IRS is prohibited from attempting to collect tax debt. 26 U.S.C. § 6502. Tax debts that are beyond this statutory period are not included in our analysis.

[53]FHA-insured mortgages may have one borrower and up to four coborrowers. We included the borrower and first coborrower in our analysis. We found instances in which the borrower and coborrower both had federal tax debt, thus, the number of borrowers is greater than the number of mortgages. For the purposes of this report, we refer to both borrowers and coborrowers as borrowers.

[54]We are unable to systematically determine which individuals were in repayment agreements at the time of the mortgage due to timing differences in the data we used. The IRS data on unpaid federal tax debts are as of June 2010, while each of the borrowers included in our analysis received mortgage insurance in 2009. Therefore, we are unable to systematically determine whether each borrower was in a valid repayment agreement on the day the borrower received mortgage insurance.

high as the rates for other borrowers. As of September 2011, 32 percent of the 1,913 mortgages made to borrowers with tax debt were seriously delinquent on their payments, compared with 15.4 percent of other FHA-insured mortgages. About 6.3 percent of the mortgages for borrowers with tax debt went into foreclosure since the home was purchased in 2009, compared with 2.4 percent for others.[55,56] The homes foreclosed after they were purchased by tax debtors were insured for $44.9 million, potentially leaving FHA responsible for paying claims for the remaining loan balance and certain interest and foreclosure costs. FHA recovers some of these costs when it sells the property.

Figure 2: Serious Delinquency and Foreclosure Rates for Borrowers Who Received Increased FHA Mortgage Insurance under the Recovery Act with Tax Debt Compared to Borrowers without Tax Debt

Borrower	Number of mortgages	Percentage seriously delinquent	Percentage foreclosed
With tax debt	1,913[a]	32.0%	6.3%
Without tax debt	50,093[b]	15.4%	2.4%
Total	52,006		

Source: GAO analysis of FHA and IRS data. GAO analyis of FHA mortgage data as of September 2011 and IRS known tax debt data as of June 30, 2010.

[a]3.7% of mortgages insured under Recovery Act's increased loan limit provisions in 2009 where borrowers had known federal tax debts.

[b]The remaining 96.3% of FHA insured mortgages under Recovery Act's increased loan limit provisions in 2009.

Finally, FHA's increased exposure to risk from insuring tax debtors is unlikely to be limited to Recovery Act beneficiaries. Because FHA uses identical methods to insure non-Recovery Act mortgages, it is reasonable to assume that some portion of FHA borrowers for the remaining 97.5

---

[55]In general, foreclosure may be initiated when three monthly installments are due and unpaid and must be initiated when six monthly installments are due and unpaid, except when prohibited by law.

[56]We could not assess the likelihood of serious delinquency and foreclosure based on other characteristics that may be associated with these events (e.g., credit score of the borrower, loan-to-value ratio of the mortgage, etc.) and therefore are not suggesting that tax debt is the only or strongest factor associated with serious delinquency or foreclosure.

percent of mortgages we did not analyze as part of this review are tax debtors.

$717.2 Million in FHA Mortgage Insurance Was Provided to Tax Debtors Who Claimed $27.4 Million in Recovery Act FTHBCs

In 2009, $717.2 million in FHA mortgage insurance and $27.4 million in Recovery Act FTHBCs were provided to 3,815 individuals who owed an estimated $43.5 million in unpaid federal taxes.[57] These borrowers obtained 3,812 insured mortgages with a median value of $167,887 and had a median unpaid tax amount of $5,044 per person.[58] Their mortgages represented 0.5 percent of the 700,003 mortgages insured by FHA for borrowers who claimed the FTHBC.[59] As discussed above, we were unable to determine the proportion of the mortgage insurance that was provided to borrowers who were, in fact, eligible as a result of entering into a valid repayment agreement with IRS. We found that three of our eight selected borrowers were in valid repayment agreements at the time they obtained FHA mortgage insurance.

As illustrated in figure 3, we found that serious delinquency and foreclosure rates for mortgages obtained by FHA borrowers with federal tax debts who received the FTHBC were two to three times higher than the rates for other borrowers. As of September 2011, 26.9 percent of the 3,812 mortgages made to borrowers with unpaid tax debts were seriously delinquent on their payments, compared with 11.9 percent of borrowers without tax debt who received the FTHBC and FHA mortgage insurance. About 4.7 percent of the mortgages of borrowers with tax debt were foreclosed, compared with 1.4 percent for other borrowers. The 181

[57]Our analysis of Recovery Act mortgage insurance borrowers with tax debt as of June 30, 2010, excluded (1) tax debts that have not been agreed to by the tax debtor or affirmed by the court, i.e., tax debts that IRS classified as compliance assessments or memo accounts for financial reporting; (2) tax debts from calendar years 2009 and 2010 tax periods; (3) tax debts that were assessed by IRS after the mortgage insurance was issued; and (4) tax debts of less than $100. Additionally, there is generally a 10-year statutory collection period beyond which IRS is prohibited from attempting to collect tax debt.26 U.S.C. § 6502. Tax debts that are beyond this statutory period are not included in our analysis.

[58]We found instances in which the borrower and coborrower both had federal tax debt and claimed the FTHBC, thus, the number of borrowers is greater than the number of mortgages.

[59]Any Recovery Act FTHBC recipient whose credit value was greater than their outstanding tax liability would not be included in our IRS June 30, 2010, file because the refundable credit would have eliminated their outstanding tax liability.

foreclosed homes purchased by tax debtors had a total mortgage insurance value of $36.5 million, potentially resulting in a loss to the MMIF.

Figure 3: Serious Delinquency and Foreclosure Rates for Borrowers with Tax Debt Who Claimed the FTHBC under The Recovery Act Compared to Borrowers without Tax Debt

Borrower	Number of mortgages	Percentage seriously delinquent	Percentage foreclosed
With tax debt	3,812[a]	26.9%	4.7%
Without tax debt	696,191[b]	11.9%	1.4%
Total	700,003		

Source: GAO analysis of FHA and IRS data. GAO analyis of FHA mortgage data as of September 2011, IRS FTHBC data as of July 10, 2010, and IRS known tax debt data as of June 30, 2010.

[a]0.5% of all mortgages obtained by FHA borrowers with known federal tax debts who received the FTHBC under the Recovery Act.

[b]99.5% of all mortgages obtained by FHA borrowers without known federal tax debts who received the FTHBC under the Recovery Act.

The FTHBC is a refundable credit, meaning taxpayers could receive payments in excess of their tax liability. Federal law typically requires that any federal tax refund be offset to pay down an individual's unpaid taxes.[60] Of the 3,815 borrowers we identified with tax debt, 233 received a federal tax refund after claiming the FTHBC. We selected 9 of these borrowers for a detailed review and found that all 9 were issued refunds in accordance with federal law. For example, three of these cases had filed bankruptcy prior to receiving the refund. Federal bankruptcy law prevents IRS from taking collections actions, such as offsetting postpetition refunds, against individuals undergoing bankruptcy proceedings.[61]

---

[60]26 U.S.C. § 6402(d).

[61]11 U.S.C. § 362(b)(26).

The amounts of unpaid federal taxes, mortgage insurance, and FTHBCs we identified are likely understated for the following reasons:

- Certain individuals did not file tax returns or underreported their income, and therefore are not included in our analysis.
- Data limitations in the FTHBC data prevented us from isolating all individuals who benefitted from the FTHBC under the Recovery Act.[62]
- Any Recovery Act FTHBC recipient whose FTHBC was greater than their outstanding tax liability would not be included in our analysis because the refundable credit would have offset their outstanding tax liability. Federal law generally requires that IRS offset any refund against an individual's tax liability.[63]

Shortcomings in the Capacity of FHA-Required Documentation to Identify Tax Debts and in Certain Policies Allow Tax Debtors to Obtain Mortgage Insurance

Some ineligible tax debtors received FHA mortgage insurance, in part, due to shortcomings in the capacity of FHA-required documentation to identify tax debts and shortcomings in other policies that lenders may misinterpret. Lenders are required by FHA policy to perform steps to identify an applicant's federal debt status, but the information provided by these steps does not reliably indicate an applicant's tax debt. Statutory restrictions limit the disclosure of taxpayer information without the taxpayer's consent. Lenders are already required to obtain such consent through an IRS form they use to validate the income of some applicants. This same form could also be used to obtain permission from applicants to access reliable tax-debt information directly from IRS, but doing so is not addressed in FHA's policies. Requiring lenders to collect more reliable information on tax debts could better prevent ineligible tax debtors from obtaining FHA mortgage insurance. Further, FHA's policies requiring lenders to investigate whether tax liens indicate unresolved tax debt are unclear and may be misinterpreted. The lenders we spoke with believed they were in compliance with FHA policies when they provided FHA-insured loans to applicants with tax liens, but FHA officials indicated otherwise. As a result of these shortcomings, lenders may approve federally insured mortgages for ineligible applicants with delinquent tax debt in violation of federal policies.

---

[62]We were only able to identify and analyze about 43 percent of all Recovery Act FTHBCs. Additional details on scope limitations related to the FTHBC can be found in appendix I.

[63]26 U.S.C. § 6402(d).

Information That FHA Requires Lenders to Collect on Mortgage Applicants Does Not Reliably Indicate the Existence of Federal Tax Debt

Consistent with OMB policies, FHA has lender policies intended to prevent ineligible tax debtors from obtaining FHA mortgage insurance; however, the information the agency requires lenders to collect does not reliably indicate the existence of federal tax debt. The three sources of information FHA requires lenders to obtain each have shortcomings in their capacity to identify borrowers' tax debts:

- Uniform Residential Loan Application (URLA). The URLA requires that applicants declare any federal debt that is delinquent or in default. The URLA also requires applicants to disclose any liabilities, including tax debt, so a lender can assess the applicant's ability to repay the proposed mortgage. While knowingly making false statements on an URLA is a federal crime and may deter some from lying about their tax debt, much of our work has focused on the inadequacies of self-reported information without independent verification.[64] In fact, our comparison of the URLAs in eight mortgage files with IRS tax data revealed that five borrowers wrongly declared they were not, by FHA's definition, delinquent or in default on federal tax debt (e.g., not in a valid IRS repayment agreement).[65] In addition, six of the borrowers did not properly disclose the tax debts on the liabilities section of the URLA. Because of the federal statute that prohibits the disclosure of taxpayer information, we are unable to refer these cases to FHA for further investigation.[66] Excerpts of the URLA where applicants are required to disclose any debts that may affect their eligibility for FHA mortgage insurance or their ability to repay the proposed mortgage are illustrated in appendix II.

- CAIVRS. FHA requires that lenders check all applicants against CAIVRS, HUD's database of delinquent federal debtors, to identify federal debts. While it contains delinquent debt information from six

Example 5: Failure to Disclose Federal Tax Liability

- Unpaid taxes: over $10,000
- FHA insurance: over $700,000

The taxpayer was in a valid repayment agreement with IRS to repay tax debts. Because the taxpayer was in a repayment agreement, the taxpayer was not required to declare the delinquent federal debt. However, the taxpayer did not disclose the liability associated with the repayment agreement on the liabilities section of the URLA. Additionally, in the same year the taxpayer applied for over $700,000 in FHA mortgage insurance, the taxpayer claimed the earned income tax credit, a refundable credit for the working poor. The taxpayer later filed bankruptcy and the home was foreclosed.

---

[64]GAO, *Service-Disabled Veteran-Owned Small Business Program: Governmentwide Fraud Prevention Control Weaknesses Leave Program Vulnerable to Fraud and Abuse, but VA Has Made Progress in Improving Its Verification Process.* GAO-12-443T (Washington, D.C.: Feb. 7, 2012), and *Energy Star Program: Covert Testing Shows the Energy Star Program Certification Process Is Vulnerable to Fraud and Abuse.* GAO-10-470 (Washington, D.C.: Mar. 5, 2010).

[65]We requested IRS notes, detailed account transcripts, and other records from IRS as well as mortgage files from FHA for 18 individuals. Of these requested cases, FHA provided us information that only allowed us to fully analyze 8 of them. For additional details on our selection methodology, see appendix I.

[66]26 U.S.C. § 6103.

agencies, such as the Department of Education and the Small Business Administration, CAIVRS does not contain federal tax information from IRS because statutory restrictions generally prohibit IRS from disclosing taxpayer information without the taxpayer's consent. Two of the three lenders we spoke with mistakenly believed CAIVRS could be used to identify federal tax debt.

- Credit reports. Lenders told us that credit reports, which contain public records such as federal tax liens, were a primary method of identifying liens to indicate certain tax debts. However, delinquent federal taxes do not always appear on credit reports because IRS does not file liens on all tax debtors with property. In addition, many FHA borrowers are first-time home buyers and may not have real property on which IRS can place a lien. IRS records indicated that only two of our eight selected borrowers had tax liens filed against them at the time they obtained FHA mortgage insurance.

Lenders using only these FHA-required methods for identifying tax debt are missing an opportunity to more accurately determine whether applicants are eligible for FHA-insured mortgages, in part, because they do not have access to certain information. Access to the federal tax information needed to obtain the tax payment status of applicants is restricted under section 6103 of the Internal Revenue Code, which prohibits disclosure of taxpayer data to lenders in most instances. However, lenders may request information on federal tax debts directly from IRS if the applicant provides consent. To verify the income of self-employed and commission-income applicants, FHA requires that lenders obtain an applicant-signed consent form allowing the lender to verify the applicant's income directly with IRS.

The three lenders we spoke with indicated they use IRS form 4506-T *Request for Transcript of Tax Return* to satisfy this requirement. FHA could also compel lenders to use this form or otherwise obtain borrower consent to identify tax debts.[67] Files for four of our eight selected borrowers had a copy of the IRS Form 4506-T in their FHA mortgage files. The lenders for these borrowers used the 4506-T only to validate

---

[67]FHA policy allows lenders to use IRS form 4506 *Request for Copy of Tax Return,* IRS form 4506-T *Request for Transcript of Tax Return,* or any other document that is appropriate for obtaining tax returns from IRS. Any of these options could be used to obtain the financial status of an applicant's account, so long as it includes the same information and provides for the taxpayer's signature and date of signature.

income by requesting federal tax return transcripts and did not use the form to request account transcripts that would have disclosed tax debt information. None of the eight mortgage files contained IRS tax account transcripts. Officials from each of the lenders we interviewed said it is their policy to use the 4506-T only to validate the income of these applicants, as this is the requirement under FHA policies. Officials from two of the lenders used the form to verify income for all borrowers.[68] In contrast, officials from the third lender stated that they executed this form for a random sample of additional applicants for income verification, but noted that doing so for every applicant would be too burdensome.

As shown in figure 4, checking box 6a on the form allows a lender to obtain tax return transcripts for applicants, which do not disclose tax debt information. Checking box 6b would allow a lender to request and receive account transcripts. Account transcripts contain information on the financial status of the account, including information on any existing tax debts.[69] These transcripts would allow a lender to identify federal taxes owed by any applicant, including debts not found on credit reports because a federal tax lien does not exist. Checking box 6c would allow a lender to obtain both tax return transcripts and account transcripts, which the lender could use to verify the income of an applicant as well as identify whether the applicant has federal tax debt. The lender may request account transcripts only for the current year and up to 3 prior years and must state the requested years on the form; transcripts beyond this are generally unavailable. Despite this limitation, the IRS form 4506-T could serve as a method for lenders to identify loan applicants with unpaid debt. Without such a method, lenders may approve federally insured mortgages for ineligible applicants with delinquent tax debt in violation of OMB and FHA policies.

---

[68]IRS form 4506-T is not used to verify income when the applicant is applying for a streamline refinance (a refinance of an existing FHA mortgage that requires limited documentation).

[69]IRS returns the information requested on IRS form 4506-T within 10 business days at no expense to the requester, or within 48 hours through the IRS Income Verification Express Service (IVES) at an expense of $2.00, according to IRS officials.

Figure 4: Excerpt of IRS Form 4506-T

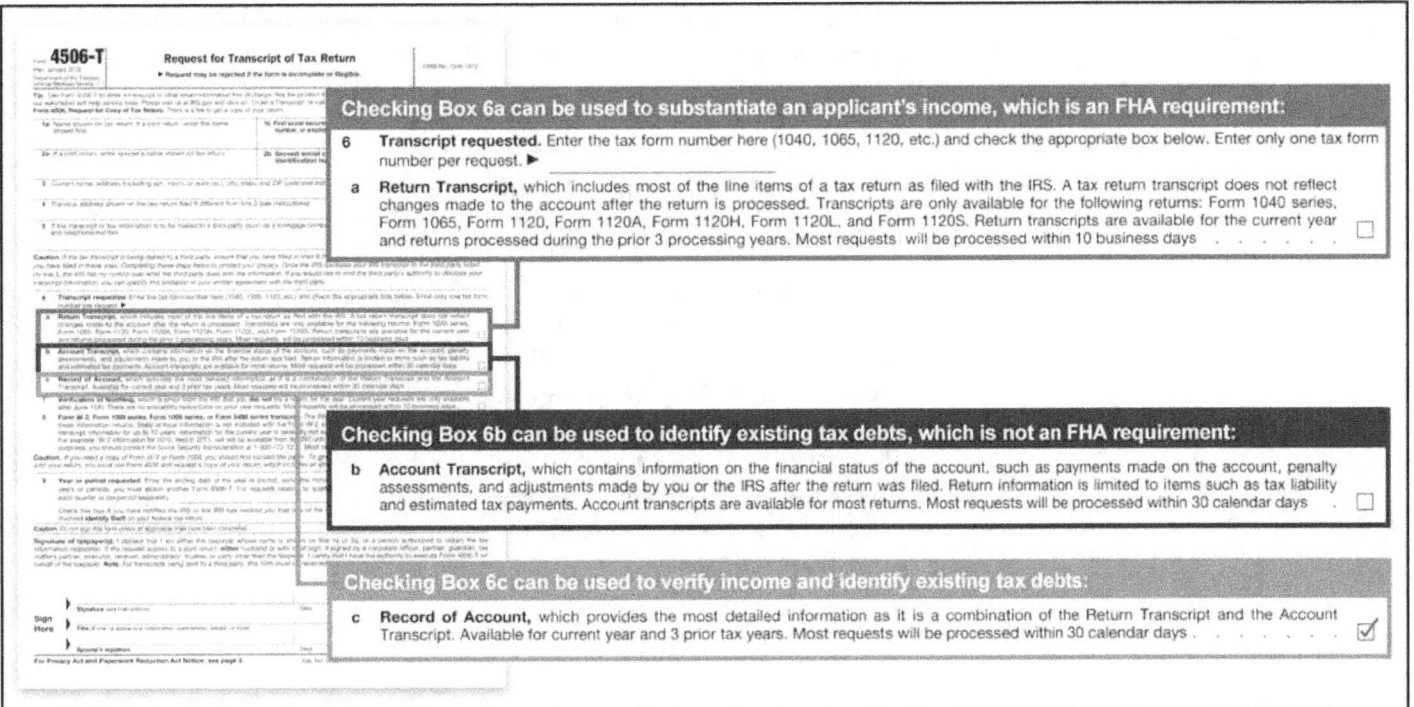

Source: GAO analysis of IRS Form 4506-T.

Note: In practice, records of account and account transcripts are processed in the same amount of time as tax return transcripts (i.e., 10 business days) or within 48 hours through the IRS Income Verification Express Service at an expense of $2.

Shortcomings in FHA Policies May Have Led to Ineligible Tax Debtors Obtaining Mortgage Insurance

All three lenders we spoke with unknowingly violated FHA policies on requirements to investigate tax liens. Federal tax liens remain on a property until the associated tax debt has been paid in full or otherwise satisfied.[70] The presence of a lien does not prevent an applicant from receiving FHA mortgage insurance because, per OMB and FHA policies, applicants are eligible for mortgage insurance if they are in a valid repayment agreement. However, according to FHA officials, FHA requires lenders to investigate whether the tax debt that caused the lien has been

---

[70]During prior audits of IRS's financial statement, we found that IRS did not always release the applicable federal tax lien within 30 days after a tax liability is satisfied, either through payment or abatement, as required by the Internal Revenue Code. See GAO, *Financial Audit: IRS's Fiscal Years 2011 and 2010 Financial Statements,* GAO-12-165 (Washington, D.C.: Nov. 10, 2011).

resolved or brought current under a repayment plan. If it has not, insurance must be denied. Lenders understood these policies to have exemptions for some applicants. FHA officials told us that endorsing a mortgage without determining applicant eligibility by investigating the status of tax debts related to federal tax liens for any applicant is improper due diligence.

Specifically, officials from two of the three lenders said they would approve FHA insurance for applicants with a federal tax lien on their credit report if IRS agreed to subordinate the lien to FHA.[71,72] The lenders believed this was in accordance with FHA policy that indicates that tax liens may remain unpaid if the lien holder subordinates the lien to FHA. One of the lenders told us that this policy could potentially allow ineligible applicants with delinquent federal tax debt to obtain FHA mortgage insurance. However, FHA officials told us that this policy is only applicable if the lender has previously determined the applicant is eligible by investigating the lien (i.e., requesting verification from IRS that they have repaid their debt or are in a repayment agreement). See figure 5 for FHA policy excerpts.

---

[71]Lien subordination is when IRS allows a later lien to take precedence over the federal tax lien.

[72]One of the lenders said they would approve FHA insurance in this manner as long as TOTAL rated the applicant as "accept." This lender subsequently told us that applicants with federal tax liens are ineligible for FHA mortgage insurance unless they have repaid their tax debt or entered into a valid repayment agreement with IRS; however, this lender's written policies show that reviewing credit reports for tax liens is not required for applicants for whom TOTAL rates as "accept."

Figure 5: FHA Policy Excerpts on Tax Debt That Some Lenders Misinterpret

4155.1 4.A.2.f
Borrower Ineligibility due to Delinquent Federal Debts

If, after checking public records, credit information or CAIVRS, a borrower is found to be presently delinquent on any Federal debt or has had a lien (including taxes) placed against his/her property for a debt owed to the Federal government, he/she is not eligible for an FHA mortgage until the delinquent account is brought current, paid, or otherwise satisfied, or a satisfactory repayment plan is established between the borrower and the Federal agency owed, which is verified in writing.

Tax liens may remain unpaid provided the lien holder subordinates the tax lien to the FHA-insured mortgage.

For more information on tax liens affecting eligibility for federally related credit, see HUD 4155.14.A.2.h

This policy is only applicable if the lender has previously determined the applicant is eligible by investigating the lien, according to FHA officials.

4155.1 4.A.2.h
Tax Liens and Eligibility for Federally Related Credit

The Internal Revenue Service (IRS) routinely takes a second lien position without the need for independent documentation. For this reason, eligibility for FHA mortgage insurance is not jeopardized by outstanding IRS tax liens remaining on the property, unless the lender has information that the IRS has demanded a first-lien position.

Tax liens may remain unpaid if the lien holder subordinates the tax lien to the FHA-insured mortgage.

Note: If any regular payments are to be made, they must be included in the qualifying ratios.

Source: GAO analysis of HUD 4155.1, Mortgage Credit Analysis for Mortgage Insurance, and interviews with FHA officials.

Officials from the third lender said they would approve any applicant rated as "accept" by TOTAL without additional review or manual underwriting, even if the applicant's credit report showed a tax lien. The officials believed this was consistent with FHA policy because TOTAL would not have granted an "accept" unless the application met FHA requirements. However, FHA officials told us that while TOTAL considers an applicant's credit score in its risk evaluation, it does not consider other factors such as tax liens. FHA guidance states that the lender remains accountable for compliance with FHA eligibility requirements, regardless of the risk assessment provided by TOTAL.

Due to potential shortcomings in FHA policies, lenders may misinterpret them, which could result in lenders approving federally insured mortgages for ineligible applicants with delinquent tax debt in violation of OMB and FHA policies. Our review was limited to mortgages obtained under the Recovery Act provisions; however, these policies are the same for all FHA mortgages. Our review included only a small percentage of all mortgages insured by FHA in 2009, and it is likely that FHA's unclear policies may negatively affect some of the other mortgages.

Conclusion

FHA has helped millions of families purchase homes through its single-family mortgage insurance programs. As more and more Americans turn to FHA to finance their homes, it is critical for FHA to ensure that it has policies in place to minimize financial risks to the federal government while meeting the housing needs of borrowers. Tax debtors who were ineligible for FHA mortgage insurance were still able to obtain insurance, despite FHA policies intended to prohibit this. Our review focused exclusively on individuals who benefitted from the Recovery Act, which only accounted for a small percentage of FHA borrowers in 2009; nevertheless we were able to identify thousands of tax debtors who obtained insurance. These debtors became seriously delinquent in their payments and lost their homes to foreclosures at a higher rate than those without tax debt.

Current shortcomings we found in the capacity of available information sources to identify applicants' tax debts could be addressed by improved access to federal tax information. But because FHA's underwriting policies apply equally to all mortgage insurance applicants, it is likely that loans we did not review also included tax debtors. To ensure compliance with the confidentiality requirements associated with the disclosure of taxpayer information, FHA would need to consult with IRS to take action to identify tax debtors who are ineligible for FHA mortgage insurance, as has been done to verify the income of certain applicants. This would include developing appropriate criteria and safeguards to ensure taxpayer privacy and minimize undue approval delays. In addition, strengthening FHA policies and their interpretation by lenders can help prevent ineligible tax debtors from continuing to receive the benefit of FHA insurance. To the extent that borrowers with tax debt represent additional risk, FHA could minimize the potential for this risk by taking steps to address the issues identified in this report.

Recommendations for Executive Action

The Secretary of HUD should direct the Assistant Secretary for Housing (Federal Housing Commissioner) to implement the following two recommendations:

- Consult with IRS to develop written policies requiring lenders to collect and evaluate IRS documentation appropriate for identifying ineligible applicants with unpaid federal taxes, while fully complying with the statutory restriction on disclosure of taxpayer information. For example, FHA could require lenders to obtain consent from borrowers to allow FHA and its lenders to verify with IRS whether recipients of FHA insurance have unpaid federal taxes.

- Provide FHA lenders with revised policies or additional guidance on borrower ineligibility due to delinquent federal debts and tax liens to more clearly distinguish requirements for lenders to investigate any indication that an applicant has federal tax debt (such as a federal tax lien) to provide reasonable assurance that ineligible borrowers do not receive FHA mortgage insurance.

Agency Comments and Our Evaluation

We provided a draft of this report to IRS and HUD for review and comment. IRS did not have any comments in response to the draft report. The Acting Assistant Secretary for Housing (Federal Housing Commissioner) provided a written response which is reprinted in appendix III.

In HUD's response, the agency agreed with our recommendations and acknowledged that current policies and procedures may fail to identify all potential borrowers with delinquent tax debt. To address our recommendations, FHA stated that it would contact IRS in an effort to establish executable policy that may identify delinquent tax debtors. Further, the agency affirmed that it would execute changes to current FHA requirements for lenders in order to address the concerns discovered through the audit. Included in its written response, HUD provided technical comments which were incorporated into this report. Specifically, HUD recommended that we change the terminology used to characterize federal tax debts. According to HUD, this suggested change would provide clarity and avoid the appearance that FHA knew of delinquent tax debts. We agreed to make the recommended change. However, for certain cases included in our review, evidence indicates that FHA-approved lenders were aware of tax debts.

As agreed with your offices, unless you publicly release its contents earlier we plan no further distribution of this report until 30 days from its issue date. At that time, we will send copies of this report to interested congressional committees, the Secretary of the Treasury, the Secretary of Housing and Urban Development, the Commissioner of Internal Revenue, the Acting Assistant Secretary for Housing (Federal Housing Commissioner), and other interested parties. The report is also available at no charge on the GAO Web site at http://www.gao.gov. If you have any questions concerning this report, please contact Gregory D. Kutz at (202) 512-6722 or kutzg@gao.gov. Contact points for our Offices of Congressional Relations and Public Affairs may be found on the last page of this report. Major contributors to this report are acknowledged in appendix IV.

Gregory D. Kutz
Director
Forensic Audits and Investigative Service

List of Congressional Requesters

The Honorable Max Baucus
Chairman
The Honorable Orrin Hatch
Ranking Member
Committee on Finance
United States Senate

The Honorable Charles Grassley
Ranking Member
Committee on the Judiciary
United States Senate

The Honorable Carl Levin
Chairman
The Honorable Tom Coburn, M.D.
Ranking Member
Permanent Subcommittee on Investigations
Committee on Homeland Security and Governmental Affairs
United States Senate

Appendix I: Objectives, Scope, and Methodology

Our objectives were to determine: (1) the extent to which tax debtors benefited from the Recovery Act's provisions for increased Federal Housing Administration (FHA) loan limits and the First-Time Homebuyer Credit (FTHBC); and (2) what challenges, if any, FHA faces in preventing ineligible tax debtors from receiving mortgage insurance.

To determine the extent to which individuals with unpaid tax debt benefited from the Recovery Act's provision for increased loan limits on FHA mortgage insurance, we obtained and analyzed electronic data from FHA's Single Family Data Warehouse (SFDW) as of September 2011.[1] We also obtained and analyzed tax debt data from the Internal Revenue Service (IRS) as of June 30, 2010.[2] Using the taxpayer identification numbers (TIN) present in these data, we electronically matched IRS's tax debt data to the population we identified of Recovery Act borrower Social Security numbers (SSN) from the SFDW.[3] The Recovery Act stipulated that revised FHA loan limits for 2009 be set in each county at the higher of the loan limits established under the Economic Stimulus Act of 2008 (ESA) or those established under the Housing and Economic Recovery Act of 2009 (HERA). Since loan limits would have reverted to HERA-established rates if the Recovery Act had not been promulgated, we considered an FHA borrower to be part of our Recovery Act population if he or she obtained mortgage insurance in 2009 at a value greater than would have been authorized under HERA.[4,5] FHA officials agreed with this methodology.

---

[1]FHA's SFDW is an information system used to obtain case-level information covering all the processes in the mortgage insurance lifecycle. The SFDW contains Social Security numbers for the primary borrower and up to four coborrowers. For the purposes of this audit, we have limited our scope to the primary borrower and first coborrower, if applicable.

[2]The FTHBC under the Recovery Act had to be claimed on either a 2008 or 2009 tax return. Because returns for the 2009 tax year were due by April 15, 2010, all claims filed on time, without an extension, would be accounted for in the July 2010 data.

[3]A TIN is a unique nine-digit identifier assigned to each business and individual that files a tax return. For most individuals, the Social Security number is the TIN. For businesses, the employer identification number assigned by IRS serves as the TIN.

[4]Loan limits set forth under HERA were to be in place in 2009, but they were not fully implemented until October 2011 due to a series of temporary measures, including the Recovery Act, to ensure that higher limits were allowed to continue.

[5]The Recovery Act applied for borrowers with credit approval dates—the underwriters' approval date of the loan—in calendar year 2009.

To determine the extent to which individuals with unpaid taxes received the FTHBC under the Recovery Act, we obtained and analyzed FTHBC transaction data from IRS as of July 10, 2010, and then electronically matched IRS's tax debt data to the population of individuals who claimed the FTHBC under the Recovery Act.[6] Since IRS's FTHBC data do not contain home purchase dates, we were unable to isolate all individuals who benefitted from the FTHBC under the Recovery Act. As a result, we used the SFDW to obtain home purchase dates to determine which FTHBCs were awarded under the Recovery Act. We electronically matched the FTHBC transaction data TINs with the SSNs in the SFDW and extracted mortgages with closing dates from January 1, 2009, through November 30, 2009, to identify a population of Recovery Act FTHBC recipients with FHA mortgage insurance. We identified 722,003 FTHBC claims associated with the Recovery Act for individuals who financed their home using FHA mortgage insurance, and in our prior work we found that there were 1,669,081 FTHBC claims filed under the Recovery Act.[7] Therefore, we estimate that our analysis includes approximately 43 percent of all FTHBCs claimed under the Recovery Act.

Therefore, our analysis includes two groups:

1. individuals who received FHA mortgage insurance under the higher limits authorized under the Recovery Act, and
2. individuals who received the FTHBC under the Recovery Act and obtained FHA mortgage insurance of any value.

Further, to determine the extent to which these Recovery Act FTHBC recipients with unpaid tax debt received federal tax refunds in the same year they claimed the FTHBC, we obtained and analyzed federal tax refund data from IRS from fiscal years 2009 and 2010.[8] We electronically matched the refund data TINs with the TINs we identified to be FHA

---

[6]The FTHBC was available under the Recovery Act for homes purchased from January 1, 2009, through November 30, 2009.

[7]GAO, *Tax Administration: Usage and Selected Analyses of the First-Time Homebuyer Credit*, GAO-10-1025R (Washington, D.C.: Sept. 2, 2010).

[8]We removed refunds that occurred after June 30, 2010, because our unpaid tax data from IRS were as of this date. This was necessary because we would not have been able to identify whether an individual had paid off their federal tax debt if they had done so after June 30, 2010.

mortgage insurance borrowers who claimed the FTHBC under the Recovery Act while having unpaid federal tax debt.

To avoid overestimating the amount owed by borrowers who benefitted from the increased loan limits for FHA mortgage insurance under the Recovery Act and FTHBC recipients with unpaid federal tax debts, and to capture only significant tax debts, we excluded from our analysis tax debts meeting specific criteria to establish a minimum threshold in the amount of tax debt to be considered when determining whether a tax debt is significant. The criteria we used to exclude tax debts are as follows:

- tax debts IRS classified as compliance assessments or memo accounts for financial reporting,[9]
- tax debts from calendar years 2009 and 2010 tax periods,[10]
- tax debts that were assessed by IRS after the mortgage insurance was issued, and
- tax debts from individuals with total unpaid taxes of less than $100.

The criteria above were used to exclude tax debts that might be under dispute or generally duplicative or invalid, and tax debts that were recently incurred. Specifically, compliance assessments or memo accounts were excluded because these taxes have neither been agreed to by the taxpayers nor affirmed by the court, or these taxes could be invalid or duplicative of other taxes already reported. We also excluded tax debts from calendar years 2009 and 2010 tax periods to eliminate tax debt that may involve matters that are routinely resolved between the taxpayers and IRS, with the taxes paid or abated within a short time. We excluded any debts that were assessed by IRS after the mortgage insurance was received because those debts would not have been included in IRS records at the time the mortgage insurance was issued. We also excluded tax debts of less than $100 because we considered them insignificant for the purpose of determining the extent of taxes owed by Recovery Act recipients. Using these criteria, we identified at least 6,327 Recovery Act recipients with federal tax debt.

---

[9]Under federal accounting standards, unpaid assessments require taxpayer or court agreement to be considered federal taxes receivables. Compliance assessments and memo accounts are not considered federal taxes receivable because they are not agreed to by taxpayers or the courts.

[10]The length of a delinquent tax period is dependent on the type of tax owed. For instance, income taxes are assessed on an annual basis; payroll taxes are assessed on a quarterly basis.

To provide examples of Recovery Act recipients who have unpaid federal
taxes, we selected a non-probability sample of Recovery Act beneficiaries
for a detailed review. We used the selection criteria below to provide
examples that illustrate the sizeable amounts of taxes owed by some
individuals who benefitted from the Recovery Act:

- We selected nine individuals who benefitted from increased FHA
  mortgage limits who had (1) large amounts of unpaid federal tax debt
  (at least $100,000), (2) at least three delinquent tax periods, and (3)
  indications of IRS penalties or home foreclosures.
- We also selected nine individuals who benefitted from the FTHBC and
  obtained FHA mortgage insurance of any value who had (1) large
  amounts of unpaid federal tax debt (at least $50,000), (2) at least five
  delinquent tax periods, (3) FHA mortgage insurance of $200,000 or
  more, and (4) indications of IRS penalties or home foreclosures.[11]

We requested IRS notes, detailed account transcripts, and other records
from IRS as well as mortgage files from FHA for these 18 individuals. Of
the 18 total requested cases, FHA provided us information that only
allowed us to fully analyze 8 of them.[12,13] Although we did not receive
complete information necessary to fully analyze the remaining cases, we
were able to assess all 18 for limited purposes (e.g., nonfiling of tax
returns). We also selected 9 additional cases of FTHBC recipients who
received tax refunds to determine how they were able to receive federal
tax refunds while having unpaid federal taxes.[14] For these 9, we selected

---

[11]The value of mortgage insurance was not a criterion in selecting cases for borrowers
who obtained FHA mortgage insurance under the Recovery Act because all of these
mortgages were as a result of increased FHA loan limits in high-cost areas. For each of
the two groups included in our analysis, we selected two cases with IRS civil penalties for
noncompliance and two cases in which the home had been foreclosed.

[12]To mask the identities of the tax debtors included in our case studies, we requested
additional files from FHA that were not tax debtors.

[13]FHA and IRS provided us some information on an additional three cases; however, we
found that two of these cases did not have outstanding debt at the time they obtained FHA
mortgage insurance, because they were either deemed an innocent spouse (granted relief
from a joint tax liability) or had satisfied the repayment portion on an offer in compromise
(an agreement to settle the debt for less than the amount owed). The third case's debt had
been removed from IRS because it was beyond the 10-year statutory collection period at
the time we received the IRS records, therefore we did not include them in our analysis.
We did not receive FHA mortgage files from FHA for the remaining seven cases because
the lenders for these files had either gone out of business or were not otherwise required
to provide the mortgage file, according to FHA officials.

[14] We did not request FHA mortgage files for these nine cases.

individuals who had (1) at least $5,000 in unpaid federal tax debt, (2) at least three delinquent tax periods, and (3) a federal tax refund value of at least $5,000. All of our cases were selected to illustrate the sizeable amounts of taxes owed by some individuals who benefitted from the Recovery Act. None of our case selections provide information that can be generalized beyond the specific cases presented.

To analyze the controls FHA has in place to prevent ineligible individuals with unpaid federal tax debt from receiving mortgage insurance, we reviewed FHA's lender credit analysis and underwriting handbook, mortgagee letters, and reports from GAO and HUD's Office of Inspector General.[15,16] We also interviewed officials from FHA's Office of Single Family Housing and Office of the Chief Information Officer.

To understand how private lenders interpret and implement FHA's guidelines for preventing individuals with delinquent federal tax debt from receiving mortgage insurance, we interviewed senior-level officials from three large FHA-approved lenders. We selected four lenders based on the following criteria: (1) we selected the two largest lenders in terms of the number of FHA loans approved in 2009, and (2) we selected 2 of the top 10 largest FHA lenders that approved a comparable number of FHA loans in 2009 but varied in proportion of loans awarded to individuals with federal tax debt. However, the lender chosen for having a high proportion of loans awarded to individuals with federal tax debt declined to speak with GAO officials. In total, the three lenders we interviewed endorsed about 15 percent of all FHA mortgages for homes purchased in 2009.

Data Reliability Assessment

To assess the reliability of record-level IRS unpaid assessments and FTHBC data, we relied on the work we performed during our annual audit of IRS's financial statements and interviewed knowledgeable IRS officials about any data reliability issues.[17] We also performed electronic testing of required FTHBC elements. While our financial statement audits have

---

[15]HUD Handbook 4155.1, Mortgage Credit Analysis for Mortgage Insurance (March 2011).

[16]Mortgagee letters are written instructions that FHA periodically issues to all of its approved lenders (mortgagees).

[17]GAO, Financial Audit: IRS's Fiscal Years 2010 and 2009 Financial Statements, GAO-11-142 (Washington, D.C.: Nov. 10, 2010).

identified some data reliability problems associated with tracing IRS's tax records to source records and including errors and delays in recording taxpayer information and payments, we determined that the data were sufficiently reliable to address this report's objectives.

To assess the reliability of record-level FHA mortgage insurance data, we reviewed documentation from FHA, interviewed FHA officials who administer these information systems and officials who routinely use these systems for mortgage insurance management, verified selected data across multiple sources, and performed electronic testing of required elements. We determined that the data were sufficiently reliable for our purposes.

We conducted this performance audit and related investigations from April 2011 through May 2012. We performed this performance audit in accordance with generally accepted government auditing standards. Those standards require that we plan and perform the audit to obtain sufficient, appropriate evidence to provide a reasonable basis for our audit findings and conclusions based on our audit objectives. We believe that the evidence obtained provides a reasonable basis for our findings and conclusions based on our audit objectives.

Appendix II: Excerpts of the Uniform Residential Loan Application

Two of the three figures below represent sections of the Uniform Residential Loan Application (URLA) where applicant's are required to disclose any debts that may affect their eligibility for FHA mortgage insurance or their ability to repay the proposed mortgage. The third excerpt lists the consequences of making a false statement on the URLA. Knowingly making any false statement on the URLA is a federal crime punishable by fine or imprisonment.[1]

Figure 6: Liabilities Section of the Uniform Residential Loan Application

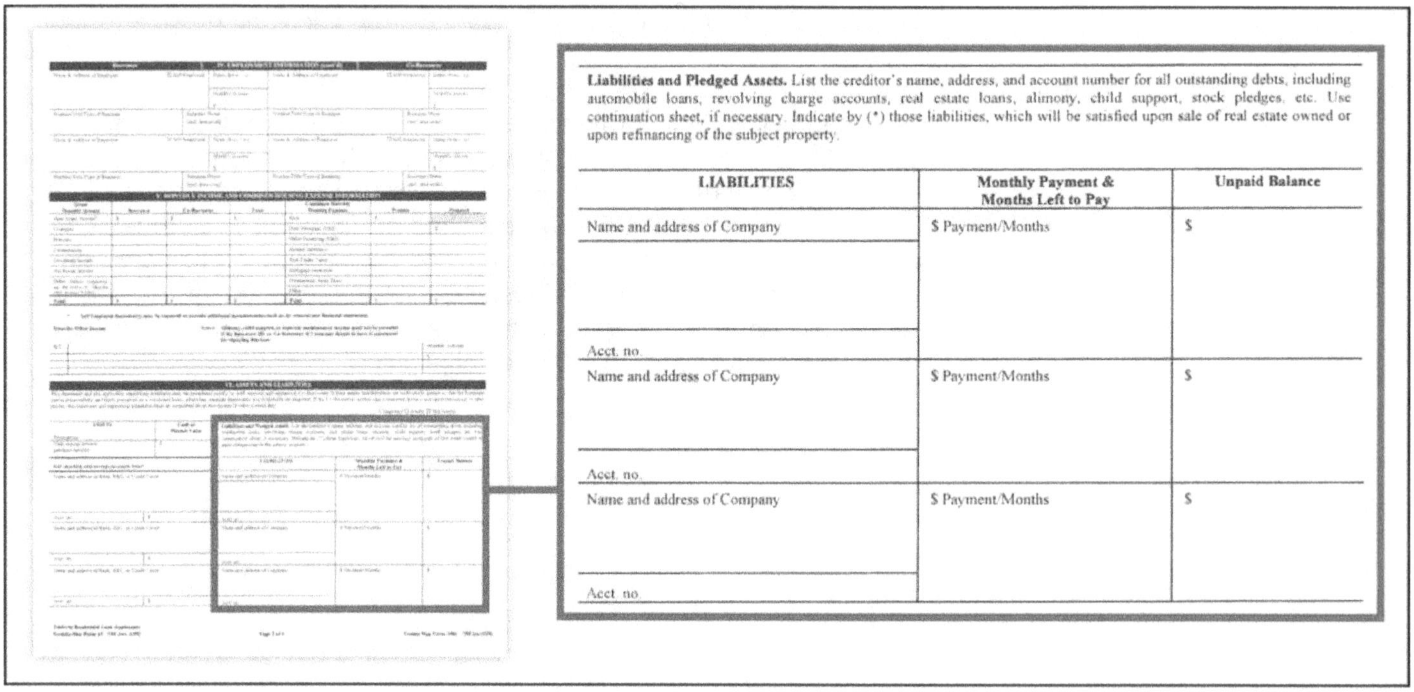

Liabilities and Pledged Assets. List the creditor's name, address, and account number for all outstanding debts, including automobile loans, revolving charge accounts, real estate loans, alimony, child support, stock pledges, etc. Use continuation sheet, if necessary. Indicate by (*) those liabilities, which will be satisfied upon sale of real estate owned or upon refinancing of the subject property.

LIABILITIES	Monthly Payment & Months Left to Pay	Unpaid Balance
Name and address of Company Acct. no.	$ Payment/Months	$
Name and address of Company Acct. no.	$ Payment/Months	$
Name and address of Company Acct. no.	$ Payment/Months	$

Source: GAO analysis of the Uniform Residential Loan Application.

[1]18 U.S.C. § 1001.

Figure 7: Declarations Section of the Uniform Residential Loan Application

VIII. DECLARATIONS	Borrower		Co-Borrower	
If you answer "Yes" to any questions a through i, please use continuation sheet for explanation.	Yes	No	Yes	No
f. Are you presently delinquent or in default on any Federal debt or any other loan, mortgage, financial obligation, bond, or loan guarantee?	☐	☐	☐	☐
g. Are you obligated to pay alimony, child support, or separate maintenance?	☐	☐	☐	☐
h. Is any part of the down payment borrowed?				
i. Are you a co-maker or endorser on a note?				
j. Are you a U.S. citizen?				
k. Are you a permanent resident alien?	☐	☐	☐	☐
l. Do you intend to occupy the property as your primary residence?	☐	☐	☐	☐
If Yes," complete question m below.				
m. Have you had an ownership interest in a property in the last three years?	☐	☐	☐	☐
(1) What type of property did you own—principal residence (PR), second home (SH), or investment property (IP)?				
(2) How did you hold title to the home— by yourself (S), jointly with your spouse (SP), or jointly with another person (O)?				

> f. Are you presently delinquent or in default on any Federal debt or any other loan, mortgage, financial obligation, bond, or loan guarantee?

Source: GAO analysis of the Uniform Residential Loan Application.

Figure 8: Line on the Uniform Residential Loan Application Showing the Consequences of Making a False Statement

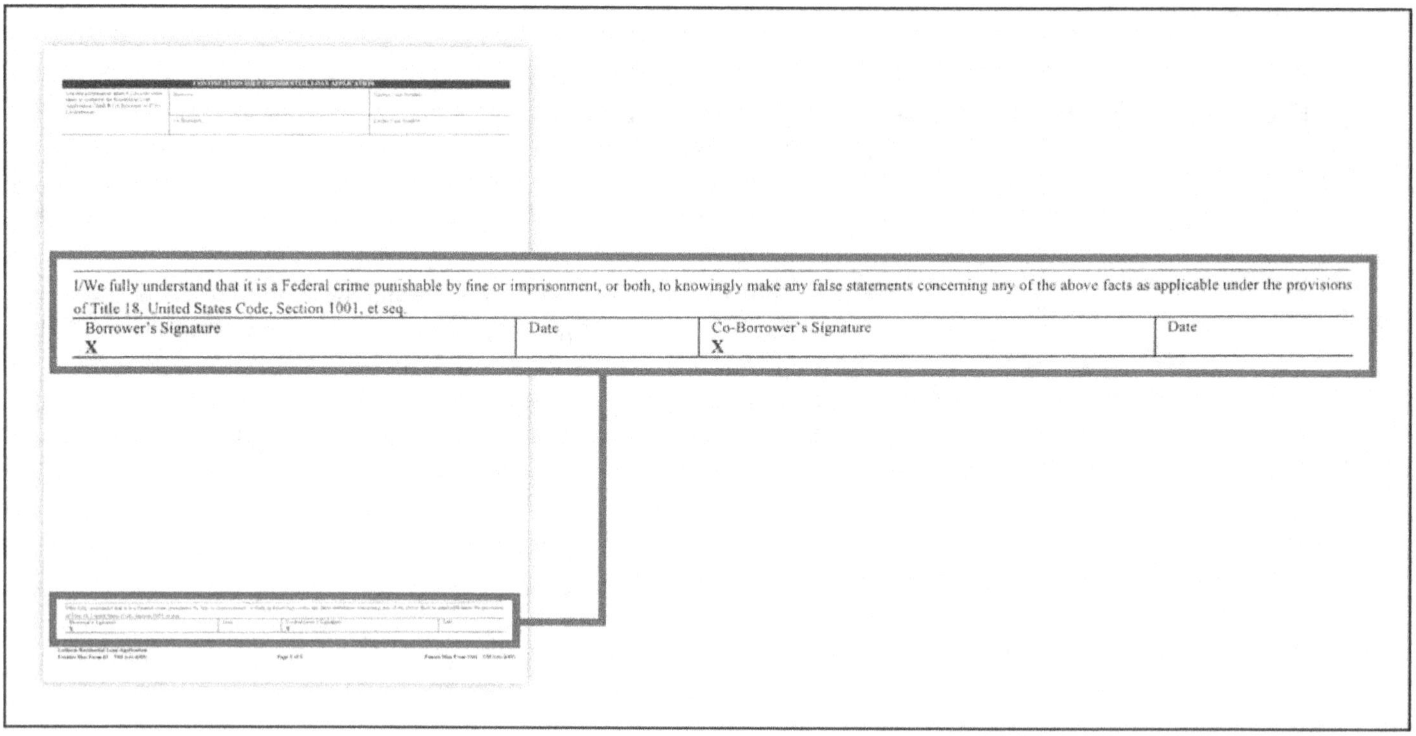

I/We fully understand that it is a Federal crime punishable by fine or imprisonment, or both, to knowingly make any false statements concerning any of the above facts as applicable under the provisions of Title 18, United States Code, Section 1001, et seq.

Borrower's Signature	Date	Co-Borrower's Signature	Date
X		X	

Source: GAO analysis of the Uniform Residential Loan Application.

Appendix III: Comments from the Federal Housing Administration

U.S. DEPARTMENT OF HOUSING AND URBAN DEVELOPMENT
WASHINGTON, DC 20410-8000

ASSISTANT SECRETARY FOR HOUSING-
FEDERAL HOUSING COMMISSIONER

MAY - 8 2012

Mr. Matthew F. Valenta
Assistant Director
Forensic Audits and Investigative Service
United States Government Accountability Office
441 G Street, NW
Washington, DC 20548

Dear Mr. Valenta:

The Department of Housing and Urban Development (HUD) appreciates the opportunity to respond to the Government Accountability Office (GAO) draft report, Tax Debtors Have Received FHA Mortgage Insurance and First-Time Homebuyer Credits (GAO-12-592). In the report, GAO recommends that HUD should 1) consult with IRS to require lenders to collect more reliable tax debt information from applicants, and 2) provide lenders with revised policies or guidance, including the consideration of tax liens, for approving FHA mortgage insurance.

In general, the Department agrees that current policies and procedures may fail to identify all potential borrowers with delinquent tax debt. As indicated in the draft report, FHA has policies in place intended to prohibit the insurance of loans to borrowers with delinquent tax debt in accordance with the Applicant Screening requirements for *Delinquency on Federal Debt* in OMB circular A-129. However, due to the strict confidentiality associated with the disclosure of tax information, the discovery of delinquent tax debt is limited under current policy but FHA would benefit from better access to information regarding tax debts of applicants for FHA-insured mortgages. These limitations may lead to the issuance of FHA insured loans for borrowers whose delinquent tax debt is unknown to FHA and the lender. To clarify this, the Department recommends that you change the terms "known unpaid taxes (debts)" and "known federal tax debt" to "delinquent federal tax debt" throughout the report. This change in terminology will provide clarity and consistency, and will avoid the appearance that FHA rather than the IRS knew of such delinquent debt.

FHA has stated policy regarding the ineligibility of borrowers with tax liens, unless involved in a repayment plan, in its Handbook 4155.1, Mortgage Credit Analysis for Mortgage Insurance on One- to Four-Unit Mortgage Loans. However, the approval of loans that are ineligible for FHA insurance may occur if relevant sections of the handbook are not read in their entirety. Therefore, FHA will seek to provide further clarification regarding the current eligibility requirements for borrowers with federal tax liens.

www.hud.gov   espanol.hud.gov

HUD appreciates the GAO's work through this audit to identify the limitations on FHA's existing guidance. FHA will contact the IRS in an effort to establish executable policy that may identify delinquent tax debtors. FHA will also execute changes to our current requirements for lenders in order to address the concerns discovered through the audit.

If you have any questions about this response, please contact Kevin Stevens at (202) 402-4317.

Sincerely,

Carol J. Galante
Acting Assistant Secretary for Housing –
Federal Housing Commissioner

Appendix IV: GAO Contact and Staff Acknowledgments

GAO Contact	Gregory D. Kutz, (202) 512-6722 or kutzg@gao.gov
Staff Acknowledgments	In addition to the contact named above, Matthew Valenta, Assistant Director; Emily C.B. Wold, Analyst-in-Charge; Jamie L. Berryhill; Jeff McDermott; Maria McMullen; Wayne Turowski; Susan B. Wallace; and Timothy Walker made significant contributions to this report.

GAO's Mission	The Government Accountability Office, the audit, evaluation, and investigative arm of Congress, exists to support Congress in meeting its constitutional responsibilities and to help improve the performance and accountability of the federal government for the American people. GAO examines the use of public funds; evaluates federal programs and policies; and provides analyses, recommendations, and other assistance to help Congress make informed oversight, policy, and funding decisions. GAO's commitment to good government is reflected in its core values of accountability, integrity, and reliability.
Obtaining Copies of GAO Reports and Testimony	The fastest and easiest way to obtain copies of GAO documents at no cost is through GAO's website (www.gao.gov). Each weekday afternoon, GAO posts on its website newly released reports, testimony, and correspondence. To have GAO e-mail you a list of newly posted products, go to www.gao.gov and select "E-mail Updates."
Order by Phone	The price of each GAO publication reflects GAO's actual cost of production and distribution and depends on the number of pages in the publication and whether the publication is printed in color or black and white. Pricing and ordering information is posted on GAO's website, http://www.gao.gov/ordering.htm. Place orders by calling (202) 512-6000, toll free (866) 801-7077, or TDD (202) 512-2537. Orders may be paid for using American Express, Discover Card, MasterCard, Visa, check, or money order. Call for additional information.
Connect with GAO	Connect with GAO on Facebook, Flickr, Twitter, and YouTube. Subscribe to our RSS Feeds or E-mail Updates. Listen to our Podcasts. Visit GAO on the web at www.gao.gov.
To Report Fraud, Waste, and Abuse in Federal Programs	Contact: Website: www.gao.gov/fraudnet/fraudnet.htm E-mail: fraudnet@gao.gov Automated answering system: (800) 424-5454 or (202) 512-7470
Congressional Relations	Katherine Siggerud, Managing Director, siggerudk@gao.gov, (202) 512-4400, U.S. Government Accountability Office, 441 G Street NW, Room 7125, Washington, DC 20548
Public Affairs	Chuck Young, Managing Director, youngc1@gao.gov, (202) 512-4800 U.S. Government Accountability Office, 441 G Street NW, Room 7149 Washington, DC 20548

Please Print on Recycled Paper.

www.ingramcontent.com/pod-product-compliance
Lightning Source LLC
Chambersburg PA
CBHW080920290526

45795CB00007BA/2596